Drip Drop

Genesis 6–8
(Noah's Ark)

by Mary Manz Simon
Illustrated by Dennis Jones

Publishing House
St. Louis

Titles in the Hear Me Read Bible Stories series

What Next? Genesis 1–2
Drip, Drop, Genesis 6–8
Bing! 1 Samuel 17:1–52
Hurry, Hurry! Matthew 21:1–11
Rumble, Rumble, Mark 6:32–44
Who Will Help? Luke 10:25–37

Copyright © 1990 Concordia Publishing House
3558 S. Jefferson Avenue, St. Louis, MO 63118-3968
Manufactured in the United States of America

Library of Congress Cataloging in Publication Data.
Simon, Mary Manz, 1948–

    Drip, drop: Genesis 6–8, the flood/by Mary Manz Simon.

    p. cm.—(Hear me read Bible stories)
Summary: Retells for beginning readers the Bible story about Noah and the flood

    ISBN 0-570-04176-7

    1. Deluge—Biblical teaching. 2. Bible stories, English—O.T. Genesis. [1. Noah (Biblical figure) 2. Noah's ark. 3. Bible stories—O.T.] I. Title II. Series: Simon, Mary Manz, 1948– Hear me read Bible stories.
BS658.S56 1990
222'.1109505—dc20   89–35131
                                                          CIP
                                                           AC

1 2 3 4 5 6 7 8 9 10   99 98 97 96 95 94 93 92 91 90

Name

Date

Presented by

To the Adult:

Early readers need two kinds of reading. They need to be read to, and they need to do their own reading. The Hear Me Read Bible Stories series helps you to encourage your child with both kinds.

For example, your child might read this book as you sit together. Listen attentively. Assist gently, if needed. Encourage, be patient, and be very positive about your child's efforts.

Then perhaps you'd like to share the selected Bible story in an easy-to-understand translation or paraphrase.

Using both types of reading gives your child a chance to develop new skills and pride in reading. You share and support your child's excitement.

As a mother and a teacher, I anticipate the joy your child will feel in saying, "Hear me read Bible stories!"

Mary Manz Simon

For Christina Marie Simon
John 14:27

Look at Noah.

Noah was God's helper.

God said to Noah,
"Make a boat.
Make a big boat."

"I promise I will send
a big rain," said God.
Hurry, Noah! Hurry!

Drip, drop.

Hurry, Noah! Hurry!

Make a big boat.

Drip, drop.

Drip, drop.

Drip, drop, splash!

Noah was God's helper.

Drip, drop.

Drip, drop.

Drip, drop, splash!

Look at Noah make a boat.

Look at Noah make a big boat.

Drip, drop.

Drip, drop.

Drip, drop, splash!

Hurry, Noah! Hurry!
Splash, splash!

Look at the big boat.

Look at the big rain.

God said, "I promise I will
never send
such a big rain."

"Look," said Noah.

"Look at God's promise."

About the Author

Mary Manz Simon holds a doctoral degree in education with a specialty in early childhood education. She has taught at levels from preschool through postgraduate. Dr. Simon has also authored the newly released *God's Children Pray* and the best-selling *Little Visits with Jesus* and *More Little Visits with Jesus*. She and her husband, the Reverend Henry A. Simon, are the parents of three children.